THIRTEEN QUINTETS FOR LOIS

Thirteen Quintets for Lois, and the

ἔτι καὶ νῦν of Grace

FLOOD EDITIONS, CHICAGO

Jay Wright

Published by Flood Editions

www.floodeditions.com

ISBN 978-1-7332734-7-3

Design and composition by Crisis

Printed on acid-free,

recycled paper in Canada

Movement One

Movement Two

Movement Three

Movement Four

Movement Five

Finale

Movement One

Eternity of line, the home
disguised, the root cut or altered—
que me voy al triste campo.
I know myself a child of folded
wings, an instant performative
text most carefully inventive.

Think again of that metronome
of particles, an encountered
velocity, a monochrome
ability almost withered.
Every point will seem destructive,
every reading an instinctive
fault, a misguided directive.

Nothing appears settled. Stars foam
from their moorings, light seems plundered,
all darkness but a polychrome
desire thoroughly invented.
Call upon that once persuasive
motion of a dry cohesive
body that remains subversive.

A sheltered mind sits with the gnome
of absence, resuscitated,
wary of what the spirit might comb
from a sacred spark extinguished.
Nothing here argues a festive
moment, or a borrowed restive
temper, wise and at once furtive.

Binu knows the geometry
of change, the stellar argument
in an ambiguous body;
the chronometry and content,
embodied in the singing bush.
A presence, savoring the rush
of attention, lies in ambush.

Let us not call it memory,
or hide a transformed element.
Binu has doffed his purity,
and that repetitive consent
he found in a field that was flush
with motion, and now feels the brush
of symmetry rising and lush.

These bones will lose their crystal fit,
that imperious clarity
of tones that ring in the body.
Stillness finds a proper spirit.

Within that body an hour
of shadow feels exact, and turns
upon that self the measured patterns
of fragile and perfect power.

Keep the heart's vagaries at bay,
its swiftness unduly attuned
to death, its movement often pruned
by a slippered fidelity.

¡Muerte a la mar con nuestros
tres arpones! Pray to the first
soeurs de charité, solid, curst,
engaged in what the soft heart knows.

We will speak in reason's defense,
find windfall and respite in storm,

and count upon the cruciform
melody in that music's tense.

These bones will transform a lost sound,
shining beyond its gravity,
and willing its own chastity,
faithful note, deep, and underground.

A small, ontological conception
has Thalassinos up a creek.
He had, only recently, discovered
a chromatic aberration in distance.
But nothing keeps him from his pulse line,
or the complementary presence of an island
that sounds upon itself.

                   Water flows
with Thalassinos as he attempts to rescue
his variable conception from necessity.
All along this line, the randy birch caresses air,
points to an infinity that the birch knows
as other substance, another aberration, begging,
if not beggaring, existence.

                   Count upon the you who counts
by empirical afterthought. No one has bought the unmarked
line celestial figures require. These represent matters
that change with the body's envelope,
and the envelope anoints its own conception.

                   We move out of shadow
into a luminosity that burns, and arises as effigy,
a fifth exercise that leads to bitterness and emptiness.
Pity Thalassinos, his inventive innocence, his arrogance.

It would take grave Graves to relieve him
of that stellar imagination that has him in this fix.
Faraday confuses him,
and an angel dancing anywhere upon a line
binds him in a Plotinean order.
He finds himself constrained by repetition,
his tuning all awry.

                    Suffer this moment
with Thalassinos, too arrogant to give in
to that sixth beat and the verifiable divinity
of a consonant chord that refuses to sound.

You flow within this densely ordered space,
in search of reason's lost coherent sign—
Lockean substance dancing with its law.
Già ogni stella cade, not one trace
and altered state that will show a design.
Gondenu: day of dancing without flaw.

You lose your place, no thought of judgment now.
The day begins as always with a death,
vagabond sign and sound of a true mask.
Such particle event will lie below
the point and state of a faith with soft breath.
Energy looks to complete a hard task.

The case has not been solved—a body fades
too soon; you spin and must feel a slight dread
pushing you out in an uneasy flight.
A febrile source of motion stands unread,
the weight of it now transformed without light.
So what of time, the village barricade?

"This soule now free from prison and passion,"
that radial conception the fabric

bears in its body, substance in motion,
cannot define that microscopic
ability that will form a new state,
tangible, fluid, touch that penetrates.

The mask will trust the bend that sets its edge.
How small the voice of the dead, of the field.
Matter will move beyond this constant pledge,
all nothingness a life that will not yield
its resonant energy or the sound
moving from shape to shape, forever bound.

This body loves its pulsing mask, stilt dance,
the thrust and spell of a pure emptiness.
Could this event address itself by chance,
describe a gravity under duress?
Who will pay attention to that art,
presence and motive, standing so apart?

Ti baw: the metronome of grace will fold
the healing bird in the bush and the breath
burnishing path that opens with a fall.
No planetary rest will hold
the logical and first touch of a death;
no falling body will resist its call.

τῇ ψυχῇ κοινωνίαν τῇ ἡμετέρᾳ πρὸ αὐτῶν εἴρηται
ὡς οὐκ ἄμεινον τῇ ψυχῇ

"El agua es la única eternidad de la sangre"
Then tell us, Empedocles, why the father of waters
flows carefully along the line of a sacred wood.
We have all heard of the angel particle,
the gest that gestours sketch
                    in their drunkenness,
a scandalous proposal, a difficult notion
relying upon a state of motion
                    no one
can specify.
Thalassinos tunes his schema, the execution of it
left numerically inexact—that fact
goes categorically underground, an infinity
of bodies in flight,
                    αλλά ἄριστον ἡ σωπή.
Does the particle wait for a current?
Such a deficient definition of law,
                    Baca's incomprehension
made celebratory in proportion, covers

the poet's fiction, never attuned to light's bending,
a semantic content it has on its own.
   The blessed event remains indeterminate.
Why now propose such a weight upon the earth?
The river here searches its own disembodiment;
Thalassinos speaks of necessary purification.
Who goes where with these variables?
Who can reason from number to number,
having accepted the water's embrace?
The water conceals that marked skeleton,
      soul of eternity.
Why remember the clear conception of blood,
or the perfect number that satisfies this
proprietary
   distance?

Francis Poulenc has a plume
for that proprietary distance,
a gravitational density that sits
within him. A singer must sing the scale
the composition imposes,
and melodies come masked and capable
of no intentional light.

But unruly stars
teach light's imprecision,
and the danger of mistaken measurements
engendered by light.

Silence will not serve,
will not shape the spatial emptiness,
or construct the qualitative movement
of a brief entanglement. Thalassinos hears
no stringy instrument, no resonance given substance
on a particle's determinate path.
Could he now encourage Francis to turn
the plasma of a familiar pitch
to the "best possible copy of a quantum state,"
and leave him standing in amazement
at the soul's ingenuity, in disguising
itself as abstraction?

The Ephesian displayed a carbon itch,
nothing water or fire's fabric could stitch.
Think of this as a broken graph, a spell

or a spelling mistake, incorrigible.

Must our Ionian always repel
a structured sun, the ready hemistich
of all event? Must one propose a rich
intention captured in a moving cell?

Suppose now a perfect and flexible

eye, something to promote a crucible
of force, leading to a bound abstraction.
ἀυτὸ καθ ἀυτὸ incompatible
prophecies, once blind and insensible,
recall an infinite separation.

An egg in a tree's hollow, a token,
finds its space, one that will mend a broken
light. You learn a commonplace lineage,

an apostrophe, a new relation.

The egg will now propose a pilgrimage.
An unqualified light seems forbidden,
yet all impurity appears chosen.
A soul struggles with that soft privilege.

The egg will have its own delegation,

lift an inscrutable calculation
from the number, one, and a notion placed
deftly in its bowels, confirmation
of distance that no illumination
might serve—a token by all love displaced.

Èṣù Èlegba has a small box made
of Danish wood to contain a small shade
—a bearded tit in its formal nature.

In our thiasos we perhaps will need

Farinata, his prophetic texture,
to uncover how infinity might braid
this event, or teach us how to evade
a magnitude we once thought too obscure.

A continental chemistry will seed

and frame a transformation we can read
as it passes, a radial motion.
The bird's correspondence must always breed
in the box an act that will always plead
a strict appearance with such discretion.

Could Faraday place a vertical stick
on the mono altars, draw the caustic
radiation into those lines of force?

Mujynya proposes a skeletal

awakening in the body, a source
systematic enough to lie cryptic,
inductive and restrained, a pragmatic
notion set upon an eccentric course.

Why submit to this ontological

syntax, a rooted constitutional
displacement, measured in the Ogol?
Such a convocation, a particle
movement Faraday might call essential.
We await a welcome to our control.

Baca recalls that first transformation,
a soul's disorder and discretion.
Could this dense soul fall from eternity

into time? Perhaps this motion takes place

in an instant of impurity:
Olubaru seeking definition,
"a rule that governs change," an invention
that colors an altar's complexity.

Must we consider the structure of space

within the body? Must the mask embrace
Olubaru's ornamental presence
and the order that nothing can replace?
From bush to village, Awa moves by grace.
There we find the soul in its reticence.

How ingenious to place these altars
in three: stump, carved stone, boliw—the scholars
of our situation, often at ease

with that open conception that will fall

toward number. No figure can ever please
dyako, its exploration wrought by stars—
signs displaying nothing like these feldspars
of musical phrase and grammar's disease,

a misapprehension set to enthrall

those who conceive life's order in the small
event and distance, a structural need.
Leibniz and our saints would never recall
such blindness, such strict attention to all
those constructive numbers no one can read.

Salamanca has moved, the soul
has become undone, lost control
of the dance, that perfect chance
of measure, and must now extol
a once and suspect dissonance.
Could such a subject contrivance
provide shelter from that fiction
of geometers, assurance
and modulated discretion?
No metrical intervention
can satisfy our pícaro.
All this music needs correction.
The village opens a narrow
passage to itself, a plateau,
a spirit, that will not console
a soul confused by time's arrow.

Movement Two

A bell at the earth's core sets
a pristine event,
a function of an alphabet,
a causal intent.

How can that grave security
construct a law,
an absolute ability,
without a flaw?

This sound in ascent
displays its early secrets;
geometry
waits for number to withdraw.

The dancing master must know
that ontological flow
of absence, the strict tone row—all by sight
despite motion from below.

Carried along a narrow
passage, a frequent shadow
rises with that motion, so to excite
a slight, perfect undertow.

Binu says a point is no
part of a line, and will show
itself time's only widow—a dark light
that might find sun to borrow.

Graph this fictional arrow,
its pertinent and hollow
substance—a virtual low, fuzzy site,
window perched in sorrow.

The graph of behave expresses the clock.
Logic exposes no external test.
No one knows God's celestial quia est.

                Sebaya
Baca lingers in his Gaelicisms,
his boat floating upon a screen, prisms
of such solicitude, solitude's dock.

                Sira
Set deep in that solitude, one must bow
To the akúsmata and must allow
a Quinean principle—filched number.

                Nafolo
A tailless proposition teaches how
to search the silk skin of sunsets, and plow
the sibilant symmetry of clusters.

                Proprietas
One learns to dress a plasma insistence
and to contradict all exuberance
for a perfect variable.

                Perfectio
Thalassinos hears a sermon silence
in the sacred wood, dithyramb substance
of Athenian absence, biddable.

                πνεῦμα

Pulse unit recitative

Listen to Danto: every idea
licenses an ontological argument.
Juan Almela speaks a flagellant Greek,
introduces Goethe, who looks down from his
Frankfurt cubbyhole on a river that no longer
exists.
Light fibers stretch along the clavicle,
a particle sounding its own determination.
You will note the paradox in bridges and wells,
the formal invariant in sympathetic strings.
And yet the pilgrim stands petrified at crossroads;
the body can give no adjectival meaning to blessedness,
offers no propositional solution to disharmony.

Baca hears the structural necessity
in Thalassinos and his soul, a possible
constituent fact the soul must surely disavow.
Who teaches these moons to generate such heat?
Who teaches Alberti to sing with Tarski,
or to go spiriting with three spiritless
μαθημάτικοι?

The choregus has abandoned us.
What can you say about a night's fall
into fiction, the arithmetic of the number, one?
Something here seems decidedly negative.
What do we have if not a pragmatist who refuses the name?

Only Russell might deny the space lying upon the Rio Grande.
Will we come to grief in Santa Fe, trying to resolve
the propter quid of Mujynya's shaping principle,
entangled in a Buenos Aires sunset?
Forget the Librarian, his shaping order analogous to the self.
Here we sit, enthralled by such concentration of form,
a Schoenbergian salute to solitude and that filched number.

Thalassinos accuses me of having missed my mark.
The Carthaginian has told me that the self
dances within a closed field, and that silence
remains an oblata distinguished by light's disappearance.
The physiologoi will not let us rest.
The Scot has placed a flowered motive in our minds.
Ignatius has composed his letter:
                    ἔνθεν τὰ πάντα συνεκινεῖτο διὰ τὸ μελετάσθαι
                              θανάτου κατάλυσιν,
a proper disturbance, the abolition of death.

Speak of singing angels . . .
Alfonsina knew Alberti blind to the red sunset
                                    in Buenos Aires.
But one might, even here, see Montevideo fold its wings
on a summer night, no more than
                        "un frío cristal de la ventana."
I call myself a guest.
I go here; I go there.
I watch the morning arrange its microstates,
and think of the common instant of black.
I need no singing angels.
All things move,
and reward me with a single actualization.
I will tie you to that social category, easily changed.
The corollary particle speeds away from us,
nothing in the frequent translation of frequency,
nothing gained by continuity, a corresponding
pattern of the singing voice.
Alfonsina knows things have appeared in the proper order.
The sunset warns against its own impatience;
Alfonsina solaces the voiceless choir Alberti has gathered.

Ravel's swan begins a song fest,
the tongue embellished with sweet sound
a poet swears to have set fast
on its best behavior—fleet, found

nowhere on earth without a strange guest
on strong, inventive, discreet ground.
The bird might tune that once swift part
just to test a complete round.

This oak structures no mask.

This maple deserts us.

Santa Fe calls itself a Spanish desert,

an emptiness never fully entered.

A purple finch rides in on a dream's promise.

With such constructive disjunction,

Rojas prepares a grave for the bird's body.

My kanaga whirls without definition,

a circular atonement unprepared.

Two proposals, one event,

and a field without a bird's intention.

A hymn must lose its cathedral plangency

to make sense of it.

All those who come seem to sing in tune,
seem to know harmony, the charts, and soon
      all have caught the sound and beat,
but you will see, hear, feel a note discreet
and all undone by some undue fortune.
      Oh, 'tis imposture all:
a gathering going nowhere of note,
a form of feeling too remote,
stretched in its skin, a perfect sprawl
leaving the music it finds nothing to recall.
These postulates of presence tune the ear,
invisible realities that clear
empty time—those beats that will never sound.
Now, think of this feeling without its ground,
linking desire to its loss,
a measured scale that nothing true need gloss.
Ambiguous Faro will not come bound,
all purity a mask
and sign of re-cognition, a bright arc
that spins a space that will grow dark.
A number will always swerve
and enact melodic grace, will preserve
a visible shaping form, coherent
metric that sings on its own, never spent.

Arising from the bush, the mask begins
a critical opalescence, the first spin's
occasion and fertile edge, a pledge
only a liminal passage might dredge
from the dead. What could this silence allege?
Radial movement displaces light, thins
a spinning body to its origins.

This dance proposes a life to question,
a story seeking purification.
Each fertile contour becomes a process,
a collision of force, state under stress.
The mask will not cover such emptiness.
Does it flow with its own information?
Deep sound, density without solution.

Say that the spirit measures these fragments
at a distance and that the soul consents
to its delegation, to a figure,
variable, changing under pressure
of its own demise. The seed remains pure;
a particle's mythic rhythm accents
the divided logic the mask presents.

The priestly poet wants to treat
the sarabande with respect, though the meter
confounds him.
            Such physics as he knows
scales through a geometric diagram—
(call it "a study in spatial action,"
propose an elastic geometry with fluid,
supple angles).
If, in this Persian example,
            "le visage du masque"
stands at the world's center,
what can one poet sing?
Such a garden of delights,
when the music lies tight
upon our ears,
            and a certain clarity
                  escapes.

What about the call and response
of crossroads, Schoenberg's assonance,
disappearance of craft,
or that deceptive conception
that will come as repetition,
acute tension, the soul's draft?

Mētis, technē—a small device
seems a scriptural sacrifice,
a welcome twice involved.
Beggars will manage the syntax,
and will propose all that attracts
the inexact notion solved.

An adjacent pitch escapes its
sound, the death bell no mourning fits,
and nothing sits so near
the metrical figure that tone
proposes to the self, alone
a semi-tone too severe.

Such graphic correspondence ought
to cover the ground the handwrought

discreet self sought to ease
a failing imagination.
Spinoza knows indiscretion
as invention, as release.

χρόνός κενός.

Does the soul find the body a fit exemption?

Such gravity rehearses a different balance.

The Saint rehearses his geometry:

Es müss jetzt der Augenblick sein für eine gerechte,

an Aristotelian craft en-acted, actual, lost.

Only Ravel could dress this singer with courage,

conceal the cricket, the swan, the arrogant peacock.

Only the vibration of another voice remains

luminous.

How clever these clerks remain,
with their positive numbers,
figurae that might explain
these intuitive slumbers.
Say the eye set deep in space
embroiders a paradox
in that constituent trace,
a measure we leave to clocks.
But Alberti might measure
us in sacrificial lines,
give us a haunting treasure
of complementary signs.
A middle note in our song
might teach reflection, empty
a proper light, and prolong
an iambic symmetry.
There the motion lies upon
Alberti's lyre and figure
the true prolegomenon
to a body's new texture.
Think music without substance,
without number, without space
—peregrina who can dance
without thinking of her place.

Guido arrives, carrying tension in his bag,
taking no comfort in his successful despedida.
The poet who here sits in una íntima tristeza reaccionaria,
welcomes him.
                    Who will ask these two
to account for the death that awaits them?
Who knows what properties the wind has scattered?
Day by day, Ramón preserves his Andalucian wrinkles;
Rafael salutes him with a poet's cap.
All these figures with their pensive women,
women who will have no chance
                    to sit upon the dolaba
and measure another's existence,
cry their purity of motion,
                              their transitive rebirth.
Dear Plotinus,
puncturing the soul with accusations,
himself standing near a dark wood,
or that seeming third dimension that needs a voice
to sound its presence. He must find a way
to mark that spatial movement,
a separation of truth and appearance,
an ability of Binukedine's baton, everything
that spills from, or into, a sacred field.

φύσις κρίπτεσθαι φίλει
given in fire, bells, whistles, a ceremonial
marking of a solar flare you might encounter
at Segu, or Zempoala, or Delos,

everywhere a paradigm of the body choosing
seclusion and alienation, a fine paradox that whispers
through the body's desire to go beyond itself.
Leave it to that singer who has not arrived
to compose a qasida,
                    to disclose
those other singers' failings, clothe them in such
descriptive transition that a full moon could only
exhibit a lover scorned.
                    Pero me voy a Sevilla,
why give in to that rapturous state of coming-to-be?
Guido wants no more of this solar symphony,
this wandering.
                    Think on it—why has he appeared?
and why has the moment turned into a fountain
that does not exist? and why does he quarrel
with Levinas about the root of home?
Qué dame las llaves del cuarto,
and give us all that soft voice of the dove
singing its sermon without regard to the parched
mountain that has captured our eyes.
Let us now invent a modulation that proposes

another harmony.

. . . ch'io non avrei mai creduto

Rafael tells himself that these provincials
misunderstand the devastating eroticism of Nyalé,
offering to lead her away from her radiative zone,
compelling her to compromise the point of her office.
Imitative Guido might have learned to dance,
but search him again in this new ceremonial frame,
the ontological frequency of absence,
where all desire marks the entrance of a revelatory
light.

Movement Three

THIRTEEN QUINTETS FOR LOIS

*You are love itself; these songs
aspire to your radiant compassion.*

1. Why should you bury Barcelona in tears?

> Orchids will satisfy
> those with a perfect eye
> for silver and glass. Years
> have taught an olive song.

2. Roubaud has brought a ruby to trade for

papers, maps and old books.
He seems on tenterhooks
about the metaphor
he has got somewhat wrong.

3. I am at ease with that philologist

who has set my domain
where things against my grain
get stricken from my list.
Where does this word belong?

4. Keep me where the rain displays its wealth.

Only the desert can know
generosity, show
itself a commonwealth,
one that promises loss.

5. Cautious, the second philosopher struts

    with her bartering faith.
    Adept at spheres, this wraith
    uncovers what number shuts
    down and logic will gloss.

6. Silly Cicero thought himself prepared.

Death became his mantra,
his own exordium,
offered to those ensnared,
faithful, bound to a cross.

7. This green is ever mathematical,

    frame and finite volume
    of faith. We must assume
    the spirit's tactical
    bent where the body goes.

8. Adeodatus chose his sign, figure

and concept of daylight.
Who remembers the slight
conceptual fracture
nothing will ever close?

9. What is the embodiment of prayer?

    Jerome's book, Pedro's sun
    or some other late pun
    that speaks of that error
    where all misread the rose?

10. Origen would deplore all transitive

relation here in this
city; so he might miss,
or be insensitive
to, Russell's sacred drum.

11. Alberti knows this epistemic mine,

 the sun's latent motion.
 Surely, such devotion
 to water would refine
 and set a proper sum.

12. These fallen leaves will engender our spring.

That tributary red,
fleeting, seems to have bred
a celestial casing
all damaged and welcome.

13. The redbud has composed a summer dance

    for foxfire and arctic
    darkness, a winter tactic
    unsuited to the chance
    conception of starlight.

Movement Four

How can the soul move counter to earth?
Prepara la barca—birth
of a spirit ladder. Death
now speaks in a beaded breath,
impurity pure as faith.
Nothing now constrains the mirth
in an altar's swift rebirth.

That binary star tells me Alberti can
no longer speak of the exact position
of Xico, and if not of that chromatic
aberration: the colors gone from the streets,
the houses. Nothing now pretends a proper
focus, even that bell, suffering autumn
air. All remains unaccountable, movement
that argues repetition or that flowing
action, one revealed only through subtraction,
diffraction, the pertinent opposition
of singular presence.

Call upon Mênes,
figure of night, to seal your isolation;
there I see your indeterminate tempo,
the fixed condition of a trace that escapes.
What do we owe Alberti whose ultimate
goal embodies his own dispossession?

Thalassinos proposes a Lydian scale,
all sweetness and order—Pythian
to the small voice of the dead,
holding nothing of ecstatic propulsion,
nothing of the wine of forgetfulness.
Thalassinos misreads Bruno, his musical sense,
or reads him proposing an accidental form.
But how small the body of those who will return,
given the sign, the design of the variable,
a form struck by the experience the Scot would disavow.
Our songs might further hymns to that small voice.
Perhaps we have learned,
standing on an abandoned coast,
the eternity of blood—our Nile with its root concealed.
Could our poet know the reticence of grace?
Could we encounter that first sign
                            no love could imitate?
All event suffers reconstruction.
All ἐπιθυμία laughs in place, casts its shadow.
This goes to the heart of things—spendthrift space
leaving us untethered.
Who will begin the fiber dance of such strenuous occasion?

The first light, a liquid shade,
has become a force,
          unruly and retrograde.
Our Blanco, of course,
would sing a counterfactual
distribution.
Who now could enforce
that embodied renegade
oscillation,
a bone of nothing sensual?

The operatic
    ingenuity
        of saints leaves Arthur
            breathless.
For example, take that
    tree, its melodic
        roots now exposed by
            a misremembered
            scale.
Gerardo must bring
    his aulós to bear
        upon a bare mode.
Our choir will surely
        disrobe a sheltered
            singer.

Alberti tipped Tiziano's hand,
giving us that luz tostada—
such wiliness in spring's command
yet nothing here speaks of dogma.

Poulenc knows the song of a closed field
that opens no ear to a sound,
buried, and unable to yield
what Francis would take as a ground.

Such instability appeals.
Plotinus now speaks to Tarski,
lingering in a Finnish bath.

What if the poet then conceals
the geologic and starchy
relations that open a path?

Un río deshabitado.
What have I learned from Rafael?
A poet marks his contingent
entrance, Petrarchan solitude.
A proper rhyme now seems uncommon,
a harmony present but spent
of such logical expression.
The body moves, becomes a rude
formality that, cambiando,
sits faultless, moon-bred, a call
of perfect angelic substance,
nature's true, balanced performance.

Francisco me lleva à la tierra de Carlos Pellicer,
to that moment at the Parthenon,
when the columns confessed their envy of ceibas.
All this drumming around a point
provokes a nausea only faintly relieved
by moving away from the point.
Such a hazardous conception, believing
that moving away from a point obscures it,

                                        erases it.
A musician would cling to the idea of remembered
sound as necessity. A melody makes no sense
"unless we remember each step in its progression,
and, once established, we reconstruct it
from the smallest successive units."
Francisco has tethered us to the reconfigured
and inescapable instant of a life at the Parthenon.
So I sit here, near Ajijic,
a cigar burning my fingers, twilight illuminating
a water that will not flow, or lie still.
Every configuration of this landscape bleeds
an intimacy never established, never expressed.
Pay attention to that pilgrim by the lake, to his voice.
You might hear una tristeza reverdecida,
and see a god transfigured by a landscape.

A resonant devastation
exalts the spirit, and the earth will turn
counter to that exaltation.

Light assumes its place, fancy stern
enough to promise attraction
to a dust it will only spurn.

The poet must think of action
at a distance, only to earn
a proper and skillful passion.

But a singer can only learn,
from the true pitch of abstraction,
a power difficult to burn.

Oh, such lyrical negation
pays in temper, or taciturn
patterns of stringless vibration.

You will go swiftly to your urn
without a proper distraction,
a state you cannot overturn.

This sound I know will clothe you in death's new dress.
No virgin, bootless, caught in the net of stress,
tells me the cruel tale I heard there.
Let others dance to the music left bare.

What might you say if rhythm will lead away,
take all your music, bury it deep in clay,
where nothing grows without its sorrow.
Time will not guide you, and nothing borrow.

Time sounds a lazy note that runs through the mind,
that point that disappears and will leave no mark.
What happens now when number goes blind,
splendid perfection set in such dark?

Flightless birds announce a betrayal—
geometrical moments, mockingbirds
set carefully in thirds, external
measures, principal bliss of four-armed birds.

Nothing draws attention to an outlandish
perfect wish, the body's once austere companion—
dominion given weight no bird can diminish,
set to accomplish death's dimension.

All our words resist a prodigal
flow, the integral and alphabird,
the blunt feel of a surd's noetic
mark; then, no interval displays four-armed birds.

Notice light's intention so to embellish
the soul's dish of ecstasies, the proud invention
of motion, the perfect point—this surd's hermetic
need to distinguish death's destruction.

La bella donna che cotanto amavi
has slipped away—so says Francesco who must give
us reason to live with sorrow and the furtive
embrace of death. Singers might know the mimicry

of passion, a depth of sign, the mark of sultry
power subject to destruction, all persuasive
deferrals and delegation, the inventive
nothing of affection testing its density.

Oxte, morenica, oxte, does the shadow
fall where the voice goes still, a lyrical
absence a singer might design, a soft design?

These unbound singers might divine a prodigal
temper, a transition with a path to follow,
touch of an instant point upon a weightless line.

A dampened dithyramb dedicates
the major; this temper lights and recalls
those bent, bound, disordered states.
Diatonic velvet becomes their veil.

Another note celebrates
the music's advance in scale,
sets convention's first detail
where sonic custom always falls.

Two notes must tolerate a third that fits,
or deny its origin,
a chromatic notion that sits
uneasily upon a line that moves.

Go further with the sound this line permits.
A hymnal necessity at times grooves
the silence in the margin
that the song always approves.

Three heavy moments on a changing line
—such ontological tolerance—
might lead perhaps to a fine
tuning, a luminous recollection.

Take this energetic pulse to define
a bright meritorious perfection,
an angelic execution,
an instrument's performance.

Say that these elements meet in the zone
of a possible structure,
sustained by the velvet tone
and tenor of a soft imperfection.

Oh, but could you dance to a singing of bone,
or count Bernoulli's space a companion.
An august voice enters to transfigure
and found a new dimension.

A wedding song sings a limpid river,
five notes in the scale of a turbid stream.
All songs in a cloud shiver;
obscurity remains an expression.

Shades of blue and green always deliver
the cloudless voice and its perfect function.
That sound might also disappear,
dancing with others, a dream.

Consider the categorematic
apple, a finite quantity, almost
mathematical, a quick
insistence upon nature's subtle sound.

These six bodies tune a geometric
rhythm to a line that brings us around
to that first intention, profound,
a full and generous host.

Movement Five

Death arrives as the body's memory,
becomes expression and promissory
note in a generative relation.
Leibniz might point to an aberration,
or scout an asymmetric assumption
for a flowing body, transitory,
an occasion for light's authority.

In Mali, the owner of water finds
a stolen seed and the logic that binds
the mask to its event, depth of matter,
true signature and motive, the flatter
change in direction, all set to shatter
the indivisible and instant lines.
Logic brings no temper to these designs.

Froissart has a smallish box
for a smallish song he locks
away; it would take a day
for a poet to display
what keeps his anguish at bay.
Jacqueline sees the paradox
in a sheltered music box.

What would be better for the soul,
if not the diamondbergs of Jupiter and Saturn?
Think of this as an imaginary order,
the articulation of a raised sixth,
a bell tone perfectly released.
What would be better for the tone,
if not a Ruggieri worked at Cremona?
We have this postulate of beginnings in sound,
the best of Santo Domingo, a proverb
                    without an end,
and the soul stands on a precipice, resonating
                    with an emptiness.
Know that you must keep close to the concealed side,
and patiently weigh its body.

Hydrangeas mean nothing to latent
spirits; all bushes seem heaven-sent.
Alberti finds roses transparent;
feels the air in Buenos Aires spent.
The Librarian will escape censure;
each night will shape a misalignment.

Cristaux lumières, notes for discontent.
Recall those hydrangeas, adjacent
to mako, a burning adornment
placed upon a curve, an astringent
turn from dogma, an honored guest nothing
will ever test, nothing will invent.

Consider spirit's evanescent
certitude parsing a quiescent
moment, the ἑις and ἐκ contingent
upon a flaring instant now bent
to expel a dangerous source, witness
an acute force, measured accident.

Binu sees a Roman element,
a bush out of phase—no precedent—
knows the northern wind incoherent.

Will Alberti remark a prudent
angel in the stone, that first mark that burns
a shaded arc, gives the voice its accent?

ὑδώρ ἀγγεῖον, shape and movement.
Once begun by naming, an event
that counts upon its own resilient
field, now flows as an embellishment
—one bereft of nurturing soil. Where does
the water coil, or reach fulfillment?

Alberti must know the derangement
of allusive fruit cups, those ardent
reminders of love, an amendment
never spoken, never broken, competent
companion to a perfect frame, a mask
and aspera flame, soft, insolent.

Consider a peacock's motion,
benevolent execution,
that takes this song's difficulty to heart.
That art performs freely.

Something always remains concealed, and small
—all harmonies revealed
only as fiction, pulse that shapes
a single sign nothing escapes.

Leave us to our self-forgetting,
a soft sound and sutured bedding,
or a probable syllable that sounds
and founds a secret setting.

What can this melody amend, conserve,
serve, if not its own end?
Such infinite wisdom might grow
from harmony's failing shadow.

Think of that discerning, absent
note, the peacock's correspondent

state, as a mathematical, abstruse
and spruce disavowal.

Mark this radiant dance, and call the dead.
Fed by stillness, all will fall
into a virtuous distress,
and sing a welcome darkness.

The hostas at the foot of the garden
speak to me in an alien voice.
The hummingbird no longer trumpets its presence.
I would invent invariant traveling from state to state,
all symmetry only a prosecution of shapeless light.
Nothing here suggests the pietra viva of a Renaissance tomb.
The body lies stiff against its losses,
all complexity set where love will not go.
Un país bien amado,
nostalgia's arbitrary dissolution, or the dissolution
of an arbitrary nostalgia.

     Go there,
under the granite slab falling flat on the ochre patio.

     Go where,
a soledad reveals its solitary relation
to an analogous self.

     Go near,
Gerardo's potpourri of constraints.

     Go away,
from Alberti's distempered angels.
The text introduces the emblematic necessity

of colors, shells, harmonies, and a baptism
that will not provoke.

Death becomes an altered state,
a familiar without an order, a measure of heavens.

λέγεται γάρ,
broaching all need in a possible structure.
Read this:
The bean bearing in its shade
an army of phantoms.
All must be "brought into shape *as signs.*"
Gonzalo's lover in motion displaces the field;
such energy teaches Gonzalo the dimensions of his bed.
Now my radial familiar insists on its place
when the dance ends.
You will begin again under the deceptive correspondence
of blessedness and a feeling that escapes definition.

3/2 Only the initiate can rewrite
the ceremony, that tone that will sound
when stillness makes a claim upon finite

and fragile existence at once profound,
a linear unfolding of a site

uninhabited by a darkened light,
or the perfect fulfillment of a ground
noetic space that must recall the right

conception of time, the wood itself bound
by the resonance of a soul in flight.

5/4　This poet tries again to establish
a generative relation that would
make sense of time as an objective
metaphysical existence beyond
change, process, event, and so embellish

the soul's enactment and that inventive
discovery of solitude's dark wood.
Dasiri might propose the perfect bond,
energy that makes absence cohesive.

The initiate knows the mask's order—
all passage from inside, the formative
decay that promises a strict measure,
the matter of the mask, nothing fictive,
the absolute object, and a substance

awaiting articulation. The dance
becomes a disengagement, the balance
that will fix a limited state, design
of all qualitative movement, a sign.

2/1   Within this space of realization,
the Great Mask might find the fundamental

process only a theoretical

correspondence, and its nesting motion
making the mask its own variable.

All language seems irreconcilable,

a shapeless sign, a configuration
resisting all logical relation.

Great Mask—curator of an orbital

contingency, a fractioned dimension
that reads sun ash and star flesh, the subtle

syntax and gift of a tensed particle.

Know the Great Mask as a great realist,
once released from passion—a methodist

in its bones. Imagine now the scandal
of its other form, the soft betrothal,

under the peaked cloth hat, to the impure,
the energy stepping from bush to village.
The word become an instrument secure
in its flesh sits alone to encourage
the fly whisk, the glass bead, a stone's texture,
and makes star ash a liminal passage.

The mask will move, and set its own measure,
formless form of all potential usage.

The dance will spin its own spine, and resist
a parodist's persuasion, the list
into nothingness, a false rehearsal
and a body without a portrayal.

Thalassinos thinks he has died, that he
has lost temporal scaffolding, the lee

side of himself. Such a geometric
proof starts a quarrel with Russell, cryptic
cunning critique, a coherent lyric
without its order or its symmetry.

Begin with structure's flexibility,
or that small but careful velocity,

the energy spent, already denied.
Thalassinos feels that he might have lied
about force, which he often amplified,
a translation of his own identity.

He treats himself with a simplicity
—or call it a well-earned duplicity—

and dances to a difficult rhythm,
a dry word he can balance on a slim
desire, all that would recover the trim
space, proposal without a density.

Could we see him caught in his revelry,
or caught in his self-similarity?

The ἔτι καὶ νῦν of shape and substance
will not leave him alone, nothing to chance;
all his instruments will keep their distance.
Take his coffin as possibility.

Mark this event, given to infinity,
and the exact account of purity.

The electron crosses no sacred field.
Androgynous Binu considers
that space the energy that tempers

all that the land of the dead must yield.
We must count the instant that filters
all "duration and space," and refers

to an invisible world, a force
impossible to deny, the course
of all contingency that will shape
an electron conscience, reinforce
all energy at a silent source.
Nothing says the measure will escape.

Can the electron body rest concealed
by movement, the root and substance revealed,
rule and relation that space alters
in its presence? The particle peeled
from open space will now appear sealed,
set, an idler that only whispers.

Binu finds a buried body wheeled
from village to bush, a path that confers
authority. These stringent chambers

of the soul must have thoroughly steeled
him to absence, given him a shield
against all ruleless, shapeless dangers.

How taut this marble hall, a master's gem endured.
Such form will always bind the body now assured
a place, an effigy, a seat in life, obscured
by grace, and yet a mark, a mystery textured.

Find me that notable and competent scripture,
such form that will escape that fallible failure,
keep us informed when all has lost its strict measure.
Nothing will tell a pure and singular culture.

How swift the fall from point to point without a rest.
Spell once again that microstate of force, what best
defines and propagates a density stressed
by sight, or sound, an alteration to invest.

What pulse in walls will take our weakest soul to task?
Why go beyond a body's sphere, the mask
that hall puts on when light becomes a masque,
itself a purity, a darkness light must ask?

Finale

Soledad me guia, field
of a still point, all matter sealed
by fertile desire.
Must the soul require
a satire
so revealed?

An altered wood must surely yield
a lost token slightly concealed.
Call the lonely choir,
the signifier
to acquire
its new shield.

Imagine a faith never healed,
its motives thoroughly congealed.
Lovers might admire
such a truly dire
force, a fire
once annealed.

The eye might shape what once appealed,
a figured image roughly peeled

from itself, wire
to a dicey spire,
sign entire
and emptied.

Invention Über Einen Rhythmus

The mimicry of natural forms does not appeal,
only a "conditioned indetermination, called
real potentiality."

The untethered spin of an original state
might become a perfect point of deception.

                                    "the act of noticing"
The invisible river finds its order
probed, correlated, a proposition
                       as a "lure for feeling."

Mujynya's dilemma ➠→ a primitive force
(inherent in every corporeal substance),
derivative force (resulting from limitation
of the primitive force through the collision of bodies)

Who reads death's shapeless distribution?

Invention Über Einen Sechsklang

Sogo bó
      fragments of identity
altars balance themselves in ponds/fields

Purification needs the wood of the egg,
its whiteness and propriety.

The Niger floods to reclaim the stolen seeds.

Andante Affettuoso

Mark the instrumental utility of signs,
their multiplication

The owner of a Kǫmǫ mask does not own it;
"the mask, through sacrifice and exacting prescriptions,
owns the owner, who functions only as its guardian"

Remember the order of measurement.

The dance, the reconstruction of event,
variables functioning as expected distributions

Dyibi-ti baw, an obscurity that denies a closure

Signs derive their depth and power by being
subject to destruction

Largo

The stilt dancer knows the dance of light and gravity.

Nothing says that any of these systematic ratios will submit to temporal change; nor will anyone committed to a system of energetic articulation know how to accommodate points "stripped of any mutual interaction."

How now address that path through which one kind of particle converts into another?

All shapers of spirit know that any object that maintains or enhances a balance of reciprocal relations can function in a variety of contexts.

Could Binukedine's baton tie itself to Parmenides' two ways, and justify the masks and performative impulse, ritual instrumentation used as empirical apparatus?

Suite

The clock drive in the millstone confirms all formal sculptural traits, the repetitive motion of dolaba.

To do away with causal equality, cause must enter another set, and disappear.

τὸ ἄπειρον boundaries created by time

The impertinence of analysis, the rescue from geometrical
intuition

Invention's trio: reconstruction ➡→ identification ➡→
production

Passacaglia

Froissart delivers a piece of boiled leather,
not much to call your attention to balladry

Mi lucha y la cuna
es la dura tierra

námurukú, inward to the birth of thought
námaraká, outward to force

"nothing does speak for itself, strictly nothing,
speaking strictly"

integration/nothingness/emptiness

Jay Wright was born in Albuquerque, New Mexico in 1934 and spent his teens in San Pedro, California, where his father worked in the shipyards. After graduating from high school, he played for two minor-league ball clubs—Mexicali and Fresno—and spent a minute in spring training with the San Diego Padres of the old Pacific Coast League. He then served three years in the army, stationed in Germany. Thanks to the G.I. Bill, he received his B.A. in comparative literature from the University of California (Berkeley) and his M.A. from Rutgers University (New Brunswick). A jazz and música Latina bassist, he lives in Bradford, Vermont.

Wright is the author of fifteen previous books of poetry, and he has written more than forty plays and a dozen essays. A fellow of the American Academy of Arts and Sciences, his honors include a Guggenheim Fellowship, a Hodder Fellowship, a Lannan Literary Award for Poetry, a MacArthur Fellowship, and the Bollingen Prize for Poetry.